Decimals

H.S. Lawrence

Illustration by
Kathy Kifer and Dahna Solar

A Breath of Fresh Air

GarlicPress

Special thanks to:
Holly Dye, Derrick Hoffman, Jane Tory, Carrie Hernandez,
Caroline Jeanbart, Susan Rovetta, and Cecily Cleveland

Published by
Garlic Press
100 Hillview Lane #2
Eugene, OR 97401

ISBN 0-931993-60-1
Order Number GP-060

Overview: Math and Animal Science

The Puzzles and Practice Series builds basic **math skills** and acquaints students with **animal science**. The Series is also designed to challenge skills associated with following directions, simple logic, visual discrimination (all puzzle assembly skills), and motor skills (cutting and pasting).

Practice Pages illustrate math skills step-by-step, then provide extended practice. **Puzzle Pages** contain twelve-piece puzzles that when assembled reveal a fascinating animal. This book in the Series features Dinosaurs.

Dinosaur Reference Cards, found on the last three pages of this book, provide further information for students. In addition, for parents and teachers, the inside front cover provides **background information** on Dinosaurs.

Helping Teachers and Parents

There are two pages for each of the ten lessons- a Practice Page and a Puzzle Page. Each page can be used independently; however, the Puzzles and Practice Series has incorporated a special feature that encourages the use of both pages at one time.

Special Feature- If you hold a *Puzzle Page* up to the light, you will see the same problems showing in the center of the puzzle pieces (actually showing through from the *Practice Page*) that are to the left of the puzzle pieces on the Puzzle Page. This feature is useful so a student will not lose the potential for the answer after he or she has cut out the puzzle piece. This feature is also useful if a student does not follow directions and cuts out all puzzle pieces at one time.

Table of Contents

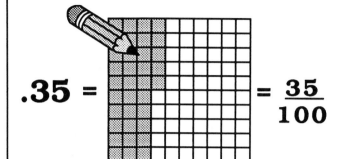 .35 = = $\frac{35}{100}$ .90 = 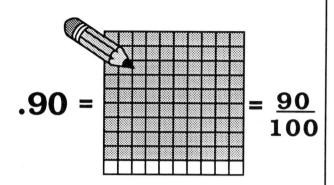 = $\frac{90}{100}$

© Garlic Press Eugene, OR

.60 = 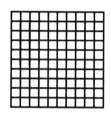   .75 =   .50 =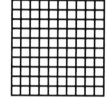

.04 = 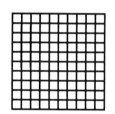   .80 =   .20 =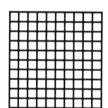

.10 = 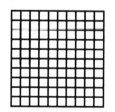   .40 =   .25 =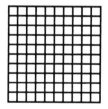

.08 = 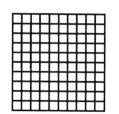   1.00 =   .02 =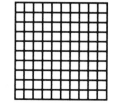

NAME
NOMBRE _____

Instructions:

1. Cut out <u>one</u> puzzle piece at a time.
2. Paste the puzzle piece in the box with the equivalent answer.

Instrucciones:

1. Recorte <u>una</u> pieza del rompecabezas a la vez.
2. Pegue la pieza del rompecabezas en el recuadro que tiene la respuesta equivalente.

	$\dfrac{100}{100}$	$\dfrac{20}{100}$	
$\dfrac{4}{100}$	$\dfrac{40}{100}$	$\dfrac{8}{100}$	$\dfrac{25}{100}$
$\dfrac{10}{100}$	$\dfrac{80}{100}$	DILOPHO EL DILOF	$\dfrac{2}{100}$

.20

.80

.04

.25

.40

.10

.02

1.00

.08

2

.01 → .01. = 01%   1.00 → 1.00. = 100%

.10 → .10. = 10%

.75 =   .02 =   .38 =

.40 =   .18 =   .06 =

.60 =   .04 =   3.80 =

1.40 =   5.60 =   .08 =

NAME
NOMBRE _____

Instructions:

1. Cut out <u>one</u> puzzle piece at a time.
2. Paste the puzzle piece in the box with the equivalent answer.

Instrucciones:

1. Recorte <u>una</u> pieza del rompecabezas a la vez.
2. Pegue la pieza del rompecabezas en el recuadro que tiene la respuesta equivalente.

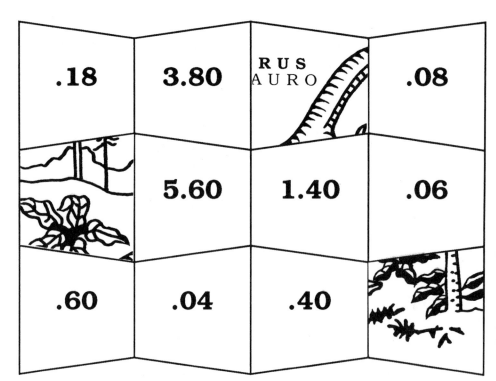

.18	3.80	R U S A U R O	.08
5.60	1.40		.06
.60	.04	.40	

6%

18%

40%

380%

4%

60%

8%

560%

140%

© Garlic Press
Eugene, OR

$$1\% = \frac{01}{100} = .01 \qquad 100\% = 1\frac{00}{100} = 1.00$$

$$10\% = \frac{10}{100} = .10 \qquad 150\% = 1\frac{50}{100} = 1.50$$

$$15\% = \frac{\quad}{100} \qquad 90\% = \frac{\quad}{100} \qquad 100\% = \frac{\quad}{100}$$

$$70\% = \frac{\quad}{100} \qquad 102\% = \frac{\quad}{100} \qquad 65\% = \frac{\quad}{100}$$

$$12\% = \underline{\quad} \qquad 3\% = \underline{\quad} \qquad 150\% = \underline{\quad}$$

$$30\% = \underline{\quad} \qquad 650\% = \underline{\quad} \qquad 7\% = \underline{\quad}$$

NAME
NOMBRE _____

Instructions:

1. Cut out <u>one</u> puzzle piece at a time.
2. Paste the puzzle piece in the box with the equivalent answer.

Instrucciones:

1. Recorte <u>una</u> pieza del rompecabezas a la vez.
2. Pegue la pieza del rompecabezas en el recuadro que tiene la respuesta equivalente.

$6\frac{50}{100}$ $\frac{3}{100}$ $\frac{65}{100}$

$\frac{12}{100}$ $\frac{70}{100}$ $\frac{7}{100}$

$1\frac{2}{100}$ $\frac{30}{100}$ $1\frac{50}{100}$

.65    1.02    .70

1.50   .03    .12

.07    6.50    .30

$$.20 = \frac{20}{100} = \frac{1}{5} \qquad .55 = \frac{55}{100} = \frac{11}{20}$$

.65 =   .30 =   .75 =

.90 =   .15 =   .60 =

.25 =   .10 =   .35 =

.85 =   .50 =   .45 =

NAME
NOMBRE _____

Instructions:

1. Answer <u>all</u> the math problems first.
2. Cut out <u>one</u> puzzle piece at a time.
3. Paste the puzzle piece in the box with the same answer.

Instrucciones:

1. Conteste <u>todos</u> los problemas de matemáticas primero.
2. Recorte <u>una</u> pieza del rompecabezas a la vez.
3. Pegue la pieza del rompecabezas en el recuadro que tiene la misma respuesta.

.85	.35	O S A U R U 'E G O S A U	.90
	.50		.25
.10	.15	.45	.60

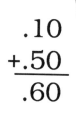
$$.10 \\ +.50 \\ \hline .60$$

$$.02 \\ +.13$$

$$.30 \\ +.60$$

$$.14 \\ +.21$$

$$.08 \\ +.02$$

$$.22 \\ +.03$$

$$.15 \\ +.30$$

$$.30 \\ +.20$$

$$.40 \\ +.45$$

$$\frac{2}{4} = 4\overline{)2.00} \quad \begin{array}{r}.50\\ \hline -2\ 0\\ \hline 00\\ \hline 0\end{array}$$

$$\frac{2}{10} = 10\overline{)2.00} \quad \begin{array}{r}.20\\ \hline -2\ 0\\ \hline 00\\ \hline 0\end{array}$$

© Garlic Press Eugene, OR

$\dfrac{9}{10} =$ 　　　 $\dfrac{3}{5} =$ 　　　 $\dfrac{1}{10} =$

$\dfrac{1}{1} =$ 　　　 $\dfrac{3}{4} =$ 　　　 $\dfrac{1}{2} =$

$\dfrac{1}{5} =$ 　　　 $\dfrac{3}{10} =$ 　　　 $\dfrac{4}{5} =$

$\dfrac{7}{10} =$ 　　　 $\dfrac{2}{5} =$ 　　　 $\dfrac{1}{4} =$

NAME
NOMBRE _____

Instructions:

1. Cut out <u>one</u> puzzle piece at a time.
2. Paste the puzzle piece in the box with the equivalent answer.

Instrucciones:

1. Recorte <u>una</u> pieza del rompecabezas a la vez.
2. Pegue la pieza del rompecabezas en el recuadro que tiene la respuesta equivalente.

100%	**25%**
80% **20%**	**50%** **70%**
75% **40%**	**30%**

$\frac{50}{100}$

$\frac{75}{100}$

$\frac{100}{100}$

$\frac{80}{100}$

$\frac{30}{100}$

$\frac{20}{100}$

$\frac{25}{100}$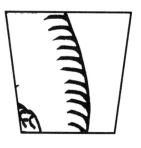

$\frac{40}{100}$

$\frac{70}{100}$

$$.58 = \frac{58}{100} = \frac{29}{50} \qquad .44 = \frac{44}{100} = \frac{11}{25}$$

.12 =   .34 =   .52 =

.48 =   .22 =   .14 =

.66 =   .78 =   .26 =

.94 =   .56 =   .18 =

NAME
NOMBRE _____

Instructions:

1. Answer <u>all</u> the math problems first.
2. Cut out <u>one</u> puzzle piece at a time.
3. Paste the puzzle piece in the box with the same answer.

Instrucciones:

1. Conteste <u>todos</u> los problemas de matemáticas primero.
2. Recorte <u>una</u> pieza del rompecabezas a la vez.
3. Pegue la pieza del rompecabezas en el recuadro que tiene la misma respuesta.

$\dfrac{12}{25}$		$\dfrac{7}{50}$	C T Y L Á C T I L O
E L			
$\dfrac{33}{50}$	$\dfrac{14}{25}$	$\dfrac{39}{50}$	$\dfrac{9}{50}$
$\dfrac{13}{50}$	$\dfrac{11}{50}$		$\dfrac{47}{50}$

$$\begin{array}{r} 1.00 \\ -\ .86 \\ \hline .14 \end{array}$$

$$\begin{array}{r} 1.00 \\ -\ .78 \\ \hline \end{array}$$

$$\begin{array}{r} 1.00 \\ -\ .52 \\ \hline \end{array}$$

$$\begin{array}{r} 1.00 \\ -\ .74 \\ \hline \end{array}$$

$$\begin{array}{r} 1.00 \\ -\ .22 \\ \hline \end{array}$$

$$\begin{array}{r} 1.00 \\ -\ .34 \\ \hline \end{array}$$

$$\begin{array}{r} 1.00 \\ -\ .82 \\ \hline \end{array}$$

$$\begin{array}{r} 1.00 \\ -\ .44 \\ \hline \end{array}$$

$$\begin{array}{r} 1.00 \\ -\ .06 \\ \hline \end{array}$$

.17 _<_ .71   1.30 _>_ .95

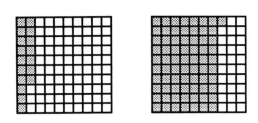 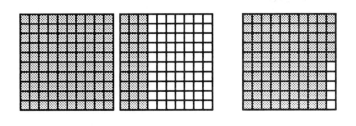

6.85 _____ .685   9.89 _____ 9.98   85.1 _____ 8.05

7.2 _____ 72   94.2 _____ 9.42   1.01 _____ 101

.583 _____ .58   .247 _____ 24.7   6.80 _____ 6.08

10.0 _____ 1.00   3.2 _____ 3.02   1.20 _____ 12

NAME
NOMBRE _____

Instructions:

1. Answer <u>all</u> the math problems first.
2. Cut out <u>one</u> puzzle piece at a time.
3. Paste the puzzle piece in the box with the same answer.

Instrucciones:

1. Conteste <u>todos</u> los problemas de matemáticas primero.
2. Recorte <u>una</u> pieza del rompecabezas a la vez.
3. Pegue la pieza del rompecabezas en el recuadro que tiene la misma respuesta.

5.6 +1.6	5.85 + .95		.395 +.188
	.98 +.03	1.3 +1.9	.21 +.99
7.4 +2.6	E R A T O P S C É R A T O	49.7 +44.5	.048 +.199

2.10 -1.09 ------ 1.01	102.1 - 7.9	13.0 - 5.8

8.44 -1.64	.426 -.179	.751 -.168

3.10 -1.90	62.1 -58.9	29.5 - 19.5

$$\frac{2}{5} \underset{\sim}{\quad} .50 \qquad \frac{3}{10} \underset{\sim}{\quad} .30$$

$$\frac{2}{5} = .40 \qquad \frac{3}{10} = .30$$

$$.40 \underline{<} .50 \qquad .30 \underline{=} .30$$

$$\frac{10}{100} \underset{\sim}{\quad} .09 \qquad \frac{3}{5} \underset{\sim}{\quad} .63 \qquad 1 \underset{\sim}{\quad} .19$$

$$\frac{3}{10} \underset{\sim}{\quad} .32 \qquad \frac{4}{5} \underset{\sim}{\quad} .54 \qquad \frac{3}{4} \underset{\sim}{\quad} .70$$

$$\frac{7}{10} \underset{\sim}{\quad} .83 \qquad \frac{15}{100} \underset{\sim}{\quad} .05 \qquad \frac{1}{2} \underset{\sim}{\quad} .50$$

$$\frac{2}{5} \underset{\sim}{\quad} .40 \qquad \frac{1}{4} \underset{\sim}{\quad} .20 \qquad \frac{9}{100} \underset{\sim}{\quad} .09$$

NAME
NOMBRE _____

Instructions:

1. Answer **all** the math problems first.
2. Cut out **one** puzzle piece at a time.
3. Paste the puzzle piece in the box with the same answer.

Instrucciones:

1. Conteste **todos** los problemas de matemáticas primero.
2. Recorte **una** pieza del rompecabezas a la vez.
3. Pegue la pieza del rompecabezas en el recuadro que tiene la misma respuesta.

.37 +.43	2.87 - 2.62	E	1.92 - 1.42
	.93 - .78	.27 +.13	.12 - .03
.18 +.52		1.97 - 1.22	.16 +.14

$\frac{3}{4}$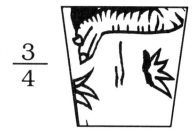

$\frac{4}{5}$ EL IGUA IGUA

$\frac{3}{10}$

$\frac{1}{2}$

$\frac{15}{100}$

$\frac{7}{10}$

$\frac{9}{100}$

$\frac{1}{4}$ NODON NODON

$\frac{2}{5}$

```
    3 3                            3 3
    8 8                            8 8
  3.89        3.89              38.9         38.9
 x 4.4   →   x 4.4             x  44   →    x  44
 1556        1556              1556         1556
+15560      +15560           +15560       +15560
 17116       17116            17116        17116
```

```
 8.37      67.2      92.3      4.54       268       .985
x .63     x 5.9     x  78     x 8.4      x .49     x 7.5


 5.18      7.82      .759      6.42      2.74       .426
x 6.6     x 3.6     x 3.6     x .57     x 6.3      x 7.5


 6.48      39.3      27.5      .967      4.32       53.4
x 6.3     x  39     x .64     x .28     x .86      x  75


 93.2      87.8      .625       983      35.6       5.29
x .57     x  72     x .48      x 2.8    x 7.3      x .89
```

NAME
NOMBRE _____

Instructions:

1. Answer <u>all</u> the math problems first.
2. Cut out <u>one</u> puzzle piece at a time.
3. Paste the puzzle piece in the box with the same answer.

Instrucciones:

1. Conteste <u>todos</u> los problemas de matemáticas primero.
2. Recorte <u>una</u> pieza del rompecabezas a la vez.
3. Pegue la pieza del rompecabezas en el recuadro que tiene la misma respuesta.

		U O P L O C E E U O P L O	
	34.188		**2.7324**
17.262	**.30000**	**259.88**	**3.7152**
53.124		**17.600**	**40.824**

2.74
x 6.3

.759
x 3.6
(PHALUS CÉFALO)

5.18
x 6.6

4.32
x .86

27.5
x .64

6.48
x 6.3

35.6
x 7.3

.625
x .48

93.2
x .57

18

© Garlic Press
Eugene, OR

$$.50\overline{)\,.5600\,} \longrightarrow .50\overline{)\,.56\!\cdot\!00\,} \longrightarrow .50\overline{)\,56.00\,}$$

$$
\begin{array}{r}
1.12 \\
.50\overline{)\,56.00\,} \\
-50 \\
\hline
60 \\
-50 \\
\hline
100 \\
-100 \\
\hline
0
\end{array}
$$

$3.1\overline{)\,.4061\,}$ $.06\overline{)\,3.558\,}$ $4.2\overline{)\,92.82\,}$

$.26\overline{)\,2.782\,}$ $1.7\overline{)\,3.655\,}$ $.21\overline{)\,8.694\,}$

$3.2\overline{)\,.4352\,}$ $.13\overline{)\,2.925\,}$ $4.7\overline{)\,46.53\,}$

$.08\overline{)\,1.736\,}$ $1.5\overline{)\,47.55\,}$ $.11\overline{)\,8.932\,}$

NAME
NOMBRE _____

Instructions:

1. Answer <u>all</u> the math problems first.
2. Cut out <u>one</u> puzzle piece at a time.
3. Paste the puzzle piece in the box with the same answer.

Instrucciones:

1. Conteste <u>todos</u> los problemas de matemáticas primero.
2. Recorte <u>una</u> pieza del rompecabezas a la vez.
3. Pegue la pieza del rompecabezas en el recuadro que tiene la misma respuesta.

10.7	**31.7**	HUS ÍCHIO	**2.15**
	41.4	**.136**	
22.5	**81.2**	**21.7**	**9.9**

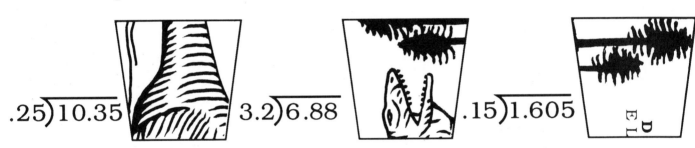

$.25\overline{)10.35}$ $3.2\overline{)6.88}$ $.15\overline{)1.605}$

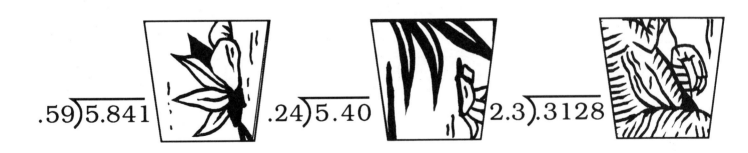

$.59\overline{)5.841}$ $.24\overline{)5.40}$ $2.3\overline{).3128}$

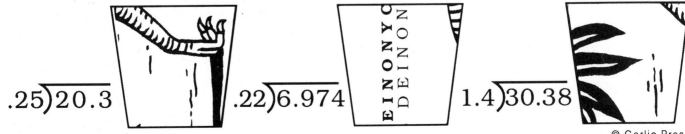

$.25\overline{)20.3}$ $.22\overline{)6.974}$ $1.4\overline{)30.38}$

© Garlic Press
Eugene, OR

NAME
NOMBRE _____

$\dfrac{1}{2} =$
- ○ .35
- ● .50
- ○ .82

[grid image] $=$
- ○ .33
- ○ .48
- ○ .38

$.58 =$
- ○ $\dfrac{29}{50}$
- ○ $\dfrac{39}{50}$
- ○ $\dfrac{5}{10}$

$7.49 =$
- ○ $\dfrac{75}{100}$
- ○ $7\dfrac{49}{100}$
- ○ $\dfrac{49}{700}$

42.5 ___ 4.52
- ○ $>$
- ○ $=$
- ○ $<$

$2.80 =$
- ○ 28%
- ○ 280%
- ○ 208%

$\dfrac{9}{20} =$
- ○ .48
- ○ .35
- ○ .45

$.76 =$
- ○ $\dfrac{19}{25}$
- ○ $\dfrac{17}{25}$
- ○ $\dfrac{19}{50}$

$107\% =$
- ○ 1.70
- ○ 10.7
- ○ 1.07

$\begin{array}{r} 3.6 \\ \times\,4.3 \\ \hline \end{array} =$
- ○ 15.48
- ○ 1.458
- ○ 1.548

$.71$ ___ 7.1
- ○ $>$
- ○ $<$
- ○ $=$

$3\dfrac{34}{100} =$
- ○ 33.4
- ○ 3.34
- ○ .334

$.44 =$
- ○ $\dfrac{11}{25}$
- ○ $\dfrac{22}{25}$
- ○ $\dfrac{11}{50}$

$\dfrac{4}{5}$ ___ $.74 =$
- ○ $<$
- ○ $>$
- ○ $=$

$\begin{array}{r} 5.42 \\ \times\,2.1 \\ \hline \end{array} =$
- ○ 11.382
- ○ 11.832
- ○ 113.82

Decimal Post-Test:Answers

$$\frac{1}{2} =$$ ○ .35 ● .50 ○ .82

= ○ .33 ○ .48 ● .38

$$.58 =$$ ○ $\frac{29}{50}$ ● $\frac{39}{50}$ ○ $\frac{5}{10}$

$$7.49 =$$ ○ $\frac{75}{100}$ ● $7\frac{49}{100}$ ○ $\frac{49}{700}$

$$42.5 \underline{\quad} 4.52$$ ○ > ○ = ● <

$$2.80 =$$ ○ 28% ● 280% ○ 208%

$$\frac{9}{20} =$$ ○ .48 ○ .35 ● .45

$$.76 =$$ ○ $\frac{19}{25}$ ○ $\frac{17}{25}$ ○ $\frac{19}{50}$

$$107\% =$$ ○ 1.70 ○ 10.7 ● 1.07

$$\begin{array}{r} 3.6 \\ \times\, 4.3 \\ \hline \end{array} =$$ ● 15.48 ○ 1.458 ○ 1.548

$$.71 \underline{\quad} 7.1$$ ○ > ○ < ● =

$$3\frac{34}{100} =$$ ○ 33.4 ● 3.34 ○ .334

$$.44 =$$ ● $\frac{11}{25}$ ○ $\frac{22}{25}$ ○ $\frac{11}{50}$

$$\frac{4}{5} \underline{\quad} .74 =$$ ○ < ● > ○ =

$$\begin{array}{r} 5.42 \\ \times\, 2.1 \\ \hline \end{array} =$$ ● 11.382 ○ 11.832 ○ 113.82

22

Answers

Lesson 1. Page 1. Exact shading of parts will vary.

60 of 100 squares	75 of 100 squares	50 of 100 squares
4 of 100 squares	80 of 100 squares	20 of 100 squares
10 of 100 squares	40 of 100 squares	25 of 100 squares
8 of 100 squares	100 of 100 squares	2 of 100 squares

Lesson 2. Page 3.

75%	2%	38%
40%	18%	6%
60%	4%	380%
140%	560%	8%

Lesson 3. Page 5.

$\frac{15}{100}$	$\frac{90}{100}$	1
$\frac{70}{100}$	$1\frac{02}{100}$	$\frac{65}{100}$
$\frac{12}{100}$	$\frac{3}{100}$	$1\frac{50}{100}$
$\frac{30}{100}$	$6\frac{50}{100}$	$\frac{7}{100}$

Lesson 4. Page 7.

$\frac{13}{20}$	$\frac{3}{10}$	$\frac{3}{4}$
$\frac{9}{10}$	$\frac{3}{20}$	$\frac{3}{5}$
$\frac{1}{4}$	$\frac{1}{10}$	$\frac{7}{20}$
$\frac{17}{20}$	$\frac{1}{2}$	$\frac{9}{20}$

Lesson 5. Page 9.

.90	.60	.10
1.00	.75	.50
.20	.30	.80
.70	.40	.25

Lesson 6. Page 11.

$\frac{3}{25}$	$\frac{17}{50}$	$\frac{13}{25}$
$\frac{12}{25}$	$\frac{11}{50}$	$\frac{7}{50}$
$\frac{33}{50}$	$\frac{39}{50}$	$\frac{13}{50}$
$\frac{47}{50}$	$\frac{14}{25}$	$\frac{9}{50}$

Lesson 7. Page 13

>	<	>
<	>	<
<	<	>
>	>	<

Lesson 8. Page 15.

>	<	>
<	>	>
<	>	=
=	>	=

Lesson 9. Page 17.

5.2731	396.48	7199.4	38.136	131.32	7.3875
34.188	28.152	2.7324	3.6594	17.262	3.1950
40.824	1532.7	17.600	.27076	3.7152	4005.0
53.124	6321.6	.30000	2752.4	259.88	4.7081

Lesson 10. Page 19.

.131	59.3	22.1
10.7	2.15	41.4
.136	22.5	9.9
21.7	31.7	81.2

Dilophosaurus

"Two-crested lizard." Meat eater. Triassic period. Two crests run lengthwise down the head. It walked on two powerful legs built for speed.

El Dilofosauro

"Lagarto de dos crestas." Comía carne. Período triásico. Tenía dos crestas que le corrían a lo largo de la cabeza. Andaba en dos piernas poderosas y aptas para la velocidad.

Plateosaurus

"Flat lizard," referring to its flat teeth. Plant eater. Triassic period. It had a small head, a long neck, and a long tail. It lived in herds, walked on all four legs, but could stand on its hind legs.

El Plateosauro

Conocido por "lagarto chato," debido a sus dientes alisados. Comía plantas. Período triásico. Tenía una cabeza pequeña, un cuello largo y una cola larga. Vivía en manadas y andaba en cuatro patas, aunque podía ponerse de pie sobre las piernas traseras.

Allosaurus

"Different lizard," because of a different backbone than other dinosaurs. Meat eater. Jurassic period. It walked on two legs built for speed. It had powerful muscles, strong jaws, and saber-like teeth.

El Alosauro

Conocido por "lagarto diferente" porque su espinazo era diferente al de los otros dinosaurios. Comía carne. Período jurásico. Andaba en dos piernas aptas para la velocidad. Tenía músculos poderosos, mandíbula fuerte y dientes largos y afilados.

Stegosaurus

"Plated lizard." Plant eater. Jurassic period. Two rows of large, horny plates ran alternately down its back. Its tail was armed with four, large spikes.

El Estegosauro

"Largarto de placas." Comía plantas. Período jurásico. Dos filas de placas córneas grandes le corrían alternadamente por el lomo. La cola era provista de cuatro púas grandes.

Apatosaurus

"Deceptive lizard." Plant eater. Jurassic period. It had a huge body, a long neck, a whip-like tail, elephant-like feet, and a small brain. It traveled in herds.

El Apatosauro

"Lagarto engañoso." Comía plantas. Período jurásico. Tenía un cuerpo enorme de cuello largo, una cola como látigo, pies de elefante y un cerebro pequeño. Se movía en manadas.

Pterodactyl

"Wing finger," because the fourth finger supported the wing. Jurassic period. They traveled in flocks, stayed near shorelines, and ate insects and fish.

El Pterodáctilo

Conocido por "dedo alado" porque el cuarto dedo de cada mano sostenía un ala. Período jurásico. Volaban en bandadas, permaneciendo cerca de las orillas del mar y comiendo insectos y peces.

Tricerotops

"Three-horned face." Plant eater. Cretaceous period. Large and heavy, the tricertops had no real enemy. It was aggressive and protected by its horns, neck shield, and tough skin.

El Tricératops

"Cara de tres cuernos." Comía plantas. Período cretáceo. Por su cuerpo grande y macizo, el tricératops no tenía verdaderos enemigos. Era agresivo pero lo protegían sus cuernos, el escudo del cuello y su piel dura.

Iguanodon

"Iguana tooth," because its teeth were like modern lizards. Plant eater. Cretaceous period. It walked on two legs, and had five-fingered hands. It traveled in herds.

El Iguanodonte

Conocido por "diente de iguana," porque los dientes eran como los del lagarto moderno. Comía plantas. Período cretáceo. Andada en dos piernas y tenía cinco dedos en cada mano. Se movía en manadas.

Euoplocephalus

"Well-armed head," referring to armor on its head. Plant eater. Cretaceous period. Its upper body was covered with bony plates with spikes. Its tail was a bony club.

El Euoplocéfalo

Conocido por "cabeza bien armada," debido a la armadura en su cabeza. Comía plantas. Período cretáceo. El torso estaba cubierto de placas córneas con púas. La cola era como un palo huesudo.

Deinonychus

"Terrible claw." Meat eater. Cretaceous period. A small, vicious dinosaur that hunted in packs, attacking much larger animals than itself.

El Deinoniquio

"Garra terrible." Comía carne. Período cretáceo. Era un dinosaurio pequeño y feroz, que cazaba en pandillas, atacando animales mucho más grandes que él.